Connie Valentine

A CLOCK WITH NO HANDS

Also by Tom Sexton

Terra Incognita, Solo Press, 1973
Late August on the Kenai River, Limner Press, 1991.
The Bend Toward Asia, Salmon Run Press, 1994
A Blossom of Snow, Mad River Press, 1995
Leaving for a Year, Adastra Press, 1998.
Autumn in the Alaska Range, Salmon Poetry Ltd, 2000.
World Brimming Over, Brooding Heron Press, 2003.
The Lowell Poems, Adastra Press, 2005.

A CLOCK WITH NO HANDS

Tom Sexton

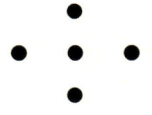

Adastra Press
Easthampton

Copyright © 2007 by Tom Sexton

ISBN 10: 0-977666-6-X
ISBN 13: 978-0-977666-6-8

First Edition

Manufactured in the USA

Earlier versions of several of these poems were first published together in a limited edition chapbook, *The Lowell Poems*, Adastra Press, 2005. Others were published in *The Great River Review, Hudson Review,* and *Ice-floe*.

Cover Photograph, "Hamliton Canal, Lowell, Massachusetts,"
  copyright © by James Higgins

Designed in Garamond types, 13/16, by Gary Metras

Adastra Press
16 Reservation Road
Easthampton, MA 01027

This book is dedicated to

Deirdre Nason Anderson

who reminded me
that we had many wonderful times
when we were children living on Oak Street

and to

Jay McHale

teacher and friend

Contents

Oak Street in the Snow ... 9
Rogers Hall, 1947 ... 10
My Bedroom Window ... 12
Rag Man ... 13
The Lesson ... 14
The Red Sox Tree ... 15
East Merrimack Street ... 16
Paddy O'Connor ... 17
Mr. Nason's Train ... 18
Poolshark ... 19
Grandmother Farrell ... 20
Uncle Paul ... 22
Father ... 24
The Great Flood of 1936 ... 25
Mr. Moore's Car ... 26
The Proper Balance ... 27
The Slap ... 28
Mike Rynne ... 29
Aunt Irene ... 30
Hornpout ... 31
The Night We Played McNamara's Band ... 32
Lucy Larcom Park ... 33
Elevator Operator ... 34
Harry Bass ... 35
Mill Towns ... 36
Grey Nuns of the Sacred Heart ... 37

White-Tail Deer ... 38

Memoir ... 39

Dark Hands Webbing Time ... 40

Trolls ... 41

Mary Shiels ... 42

On Milltown Boulevard ... 43

The Flight ... 44

Snooker ... 45

Pheasants ... 46

Butcher Shop ... 47

Great Blue Heron ... 48

Waitresses ... 49

Lower Belvedere ... 50

Utopia ... 51

Driving North ... 52

Climbing March Hill ... 53

Laundry Workers ... 54

Ducharme ... 55

Visions of Gerard at the Kerouac Monument ... 56

Lowell's Irish Mickey Ward ... 57

Shadbush ... 58

On the Dennys River ... 59

Hoare's Fish Market ... 60

Sunday Morning ... 61

Forsythia ... 62

Pollywog Pond ... 63

At the End ... 64

Oak Street in the Snow

I watch my father sliding down the hill
to our new house. He has let himself slide
like a child who is convinced he cannot fall
but will lift off from the ground and fly
in a wide circle over the house like a witch.
He went out to buy the proper tools to open
a hollow-sounding wall in the kitchen.
He has a hunch it holds a beehive oven.
By dark, he has found his El Dorado:
the oven and a bean pot holding a coin.
He tells me how he slid home in the snow.
I buzz in his lap. He is not annoyed.
He will not die in a flophouse "around noon."
Not while I hold him fast in that room.

Rogers Hall, 1947

For Anne Sexton

One night we climbed the high fence
and ran across the endless lawn
of Rogers Hall that we knew
was a boarding school for rich girls
who did "it" in the back of taxi cabs.

We ran from tree to tree toward
the building with the swimming pool
where older boys from the neighborhood
had seen girls swimming in the nude.
The watchman caught us soon enough.

Was that you, white-capped and sleek,
slicing through the blue-green water,
the one who saw us at the window,
or were you in your room writing poems
your mother claimed you plagiarized?

We swam all summer in the canals
you had to cross to get downtown.
That year, a girl caught her foot
in a mattress spring on the bottom
of the one where she was diving.

People watched her from the bridge,
hands waving just below the surface

until she turned away from them
as if embarrassed. Her body was
as white as new snow on the bank.

She was a pieceworker who slipped
away from work to swim that afternoon.
Did you know? Would it have mattered?
Despair like water seeks its own level.
You dove too deep and it was waiting.

My Bedroom Window

When I woke, the arrow in the stove's gauge
was one of Robin Hood's fallen from its quiver.
No kerosene. My parents had forgotten to pay.
The icy window would be my book that winter.
I would test myself and emerge a man of steel.
I watched poor Nanook armed with a harpoon
inching across black ice toward a seal.
I traveled with Perry beneath an Arctic moon.

I was one of the bravest of brave Shackleton's
crew, locked in a world of endless ice.
The bones in my hands froze to the quick.
If I were to die, I would go with only a sigh.
Still, I was sad when I woke to a clear window
and a sapling unbending like an archer's bow.

Rag Man

I wake to the sound of birds outside
my bedroom window. The air is sweet
with the scent of rain and blossoms
opening. And then I hear the odd clack
of wheels on cobbles, and I think again
of the grainy news reel and somber
voice saying "most of Europe's Jews
perished." "Pray for the conversion of
the Jews," the priest in the pulpit said.
"They killed Christ and have the devil's
tail beneath their coats." Mulligan said
he heard someone say that to his father.
I watch the rag man, scarecrow-thin,
below me on the street. No horns. No tail.
He gets down and takes something from
his pocket for his horse and then goes on,
the wet cobbles like skulls in his wake.

The Lesson

If you hear someone coming up the stairs
tilt the back of the chair beneath the doorknob
because the lock will not hold if pushed
with any force, do not answer even to
a friendly voice for it could be that man
come to take back our new couch
he must have missed our payment
or it could be the sheriff with another
piece of paper to pester your father,
stay in shadow away from the windows
even the one with the curtain for an hour
and if you see them on the street
cross over to the other side, be invisible
like the white rabbit in the magician's hat
and the Holy Ghost who watches over us.

The Red Sox Tree

It seemed to take all morning to go around
the massive trunk of that ancient beech.
Almost eight, I kept one eye on the ground
as I climbed as high as I could reach.
A vet who'd fought on Iwo Jima carved
their line-up where the branches thinned,
far above the last initials in their heart,
where the air was always cold on the skin.
Climbing to it was my goal that summer,
and on the Fourth I was almost there
when I was forced back down by thunder
and lightning close enough to singe my hair.
Safe at home behind my bedroom door,
I chanted Williams, Pesky, and Bobby Doerr.

East Merrimack Street

I'm far too young to know of acrophobia
as I approach a bridge I'm afraid to cross.
I know I'll fall into the river and be lost
swept away by the rapids roaring below.

When I reach the bridge, I say the names
carved on the building I just walked past.
Magic words I tell myself, from first to last.
Tripoli, Trenton, Shiloh, and *Lundy's Lane.*

I shut my eyes tight and grip the rail.
Trenton. My hands are wet and cold.
Shiloh. No turtle ever moved so slow.
They won't find enough of me to fill a pail.

My hand grips air, and I open my eyes.
Tripoli, Lundy's Lane. I'm on the other side.

Paddy O'Connor

"We go because he's cheap" my father said,
but I'd heard he was a gunman for the IRA.
The English had put a price on his head
so big it would tempt even a brother.
They sent him to Lowell to be a barber
which explained why one of your ears
always seemed much lower than the other
when he spun you around to the mirror.

A dark man in a cloth cap was always there
watching Paddy sharpen his straight razor.
They pretended to talk of what they would do
if they won the Irish Sweepstakes. I knew better.
One word to me and I'd stand all day near
the window waiting for the hated English to appear.

Mr. Nason's Train

On Christmas Eve of the year Mr. Nason
came home from the Aleutian Islands,
where he was fighting the Japs who died
like rats deep in their booby trapped caves,
he set up track in every room and gable
of his house. His wife watched with a sigh.
Was he a boy again watching the sky
tilt as the train pulled out of the station?

Twice sent to my room, I couldn't sleep
a wink, so I got out of bed in the dark
and watched for a sleigh from my window.
I could see his engine climbing a steep
grade toward a constellation of stars
pasted to the ceiling. I watched him go.

Poolshark

He was an ancient gambler
long banished from the window table
where the game became a way of life.
Dim-eyed and reptilian, Willie Provencher
sat on his favorite bench near the door
and scanned the murky room for fish.
We came duck-tailed and dumb
from school to lose at nine ball
to that dank and wrinkled shark
who held a dime store magnifying glass
against one eye to line his shots
before he ran the table.
He took our quarters one by one.

A fingerling anxious for the light,
I left that world. There's no small change
in this Alaskan city where I live.
You can see earth's inviting bend toward Asia,
and at times the coastal mountains buckle
clouds that form a vast and empty moonlit
tent above us. At times, I long
to shine like bait in Willie's hand.

Grandmother Farrell

Memory is as
fragile and thin
as the shell
of a china cup
held to the light
by a curious child,
but I see you
clearly tonight
at your kitchen table
between Madeline,
your daughter who
saved for years
to buy a failing
garage on a blind
curve with her
husband, Dusty True,
and my mother who
has yet to begin
her dark descent.

You are reading
the leaves on
the bottom of
my mother's cup
of tea, and
we are resting
on your couch,
my long-legged

sister, who does
not know our
cousins call her
Raggedy Ann,
and me holding
your rosary
between two fingers.
I am trying
to count the beads,
but I cannot
get beyond seven,
so I watch
you as you find
a pattern in the leaves,
your voice too
low for me to hear.

Walking home with
the sound of the river
on the air, our
beautiful auburn-
haired mother
weaves a tale
of a small house
with a peach
tree in the back
and a car by the curb—
above us, the innocent
moon you summoned
from the dark.

Uncle Paul

I still remember walking with him
and my father in the warehouse
on Suffolk Street where Paul worked.
The three of us made the rounds
checking doors and punching time clocks.

Few mills where left by the time I was seven.
Paul would sit in our front room for hours
with my father talking of moving to Arizona
or Alaska. By the end of August, he was dead.
He fell and broke his neck while picking apples.

The other pickers weren't the least surprised.
They thought he was strange at best.
He picked only the best apples
and left row after row half empty.
The boss would have let him go by Friday.

Sometimes when the autumn air
pricks my skin like a baling hook,
I can see my Uncle Paul. It's Sunday.
He's sitting in the ancient Hupmobile
he bought somewhere for fifteen dollars.
His pockets are stuffed with juicy apples.

Beside him on the seat is an open map.
His route west is marked with dark lines
as thick as the veins on the back of his hands.

Father

When the clerk after last week's rent
forced the door, it was almost
too late for the undertaker's

gaudy art. He left little behind
that day his death became official:
a razor and two crumpled

dollar bills. Crossing the Textile
Avenue Bridge after his hasty
wake, I watch a sad moon drag

its empty net across the river
and remember the night a bartender
told me my father wanted to be

a tenor. I never heard him sing.
Once, behind the mills where I fished
for carp to sell to Polish women,

I hooked a speckled fish
Leo Paradise called a trout
before it slipped the hook

and fell back to the sluggish water.
A bright fish that made me want to sing.
Father, soon I will believe that fish was you.

The Great Flood of 1936

It happened four years before I was born
and even then it was talked about as if
it were a biblical event. A half-empty fifth
and my uncle would say, "Water rushed down
from the mountains. The whole valley drowned."
And it did. The best bloodhound couldn't sniff
out dry land. The high falls became a riffle,
and the river drowned out every other sound.

A table came rushing by with supper on it
followed by a child's coffin. My father always
told the story of the man who was holding
on to a house when it hit a bridge and split.
Somehow he climbed to the top of the bridge
and looking down, like Noah, spit into the flood.

Mr. Moore's Car

It was painted the color of calf's liver
and might have been a hearse when new.
Every Sunday after Mass, Mr. Moore
adjusted the rear and side-view mirrors
and practiced backing into a space
on the empty street before his house
with his wife watching from their window.

Satisfied it was parallel to the curb,
he wiped it down as if it were the pony
he rode in Ireland when he was a boy,
then he locked it up and checked the trunk.
At night, we would see his profile behind
lace curtains like a priest's behind a screen,
a priest who knows sinners roam the streets.

The Proper Balance

On those summer mornings when my father
was out of work, we would get up before
dawn to look for scrap metal
thrown out in the better neighborhoods.
Sometimes the cobblestones were
wet with rain as we drove from
block to block in his old Cadillac
that was always for sale. You could
see the road through holes in the floor.
One morning we found an ancient
water heater that made the junkman's
scale moan as he added weight
upon weight to get the proper balance,
complaining all the time that he
could not afford to pay such prices
for nothing more than lead and copper.

On the drive home that morning
the river was clear of tannery dye
and the car's radio stayed on even
when we hit a hole that shook the frame.
When Father James, our landlord,
came calling after saying Mass
the rent was paid on time for once,
and the wine we kept for company
stayed quiet in its bottle.

The Slap

That morning, I put on my mother's dress
and heels and smeared lipstick on my face
the way I'd seen beloved Uncle Milty do
on the neighbor's t.v. before I hurried
down the stairs to try to make her smile.
One slap and an angry "take it off now."
Nothing more. Wearing a dress must be
a serious sin, I thought, one I didn't know.

With thunder in my head, I ran and ran
trying not to step on a single crack
afraid I'd break my mother's back
and I'd hurt her far too much already.
My mother never mentioned the dress again.
But I knew the ice we skated on was always thin.

Mike Rynne

The bathhouse and a race are named for him
now, but I remember a man well past his prime
who towed a boat with seven hefty friends in it
across the Merrimack River. They made it rise.
My father said he trained on raw oysters
washed down with whiskey if someone stood
the bill or drank to our boys fighting in Korea.
An Irishman welcome in every neighborhood.
His friends tightened the thick leather harness
before he began to swim. I stood on the far bank
with my father, and all we could see were arms
rising white from water that was murky and rank.
And then he stood there massive in the shallows
and nothing at all could make the day ring hollow.

Aunt Irene

She rose before dawn in the small house
where she raised her brothers and sisters
and climbed the steep hill that led to Mrs.
Costello's kitchen day after day without
complaint. If she bent to hold us close,
lilac scented her blouse, and a fine mist
of lilac filled her house. Radiators hissed
welcome when we appeared out of the cold.
We waited for her to come down at night
with something for us from that ample kitchen.
A jar from S.S. Pierce with a lion on the label,
I hoped. Some nights I turned on all the lights
to help her find her way down through the mist
that rose from the river, thick as that lion's mane.

Hornpout

Moving my father's flashlight back and forth
over the wet grass, I looked for nightcrawlers
that were too far out of their holes to go back
down when they sensed I was approaching.
Tomorrow I would catch my first hornpout
in a deep pool a little below the tannery,
a place where black snakes warmed themselves
on the rocks. It was best to go before dark.

While I waited nervously for my bobber to go
under, I thought of the horns around its mouth.
I'd been told they would cut me to the bone,
but what I remember now is the color of its belly
when it rolled and tried to go back to the bottom.
Moon-yellow. Cream on the top of the milkman's bottle.

The Night We Played McNamara's Band

Even Marilyn Q who would never be
graceful didn't stumble when we took our
places on the stage, nor did Martha D
who was painfully shy and thin as a sliver.

On my left was lanky Rita McG
who became the girlfriend of a killer.
She held my hand to calm my shaking knees.
Leo P's cowlick stood up like a hurdle.

When Sister R signaled from her seat
we put lips to combs covered with waxed paper.
Her foot tapped one, two, three, one, two, three.
A whispered "play as one" promised ice cream later.

And who in that parish hall was not amazed
when a passable harmony rose from that stage?

Lucy Larcom Park

Leaving the boarding house run by her mother
she walked the wide avenue to the mill
pausing to smile at a girl listening to the trill
of a robin. They wrote verse for each other
at the end of the day, counting out meter
on bobbin-weary fingers. Which syllables
should be stressed, which bent to their will?
Would her humble verse please Mr. Whittier?

Or so I imagined her as I walked through
the park thinking of her so I would forget
the wrecker's ball turning the mills to dust.
"Lowell goes in a loom and Lynn in a shoe"
sage Emerson wrote. But witty trope or not
in the end what doesn't fall will rust.

Elevator Operator

Someone jacked off on a nurse's uniform
late one night, so I had to take a lie detector
test or be fired. One janitor went home.
I passed. Boss' nephew the one with the fat neck
confessed. Those cars took skill. I'm no clown.
Christmas after Christmas, drunken partygoers
slurring "this job must have its ups and downs"
needed my arm in getting out the door.
They forgot my name by New Year's Eve.
One day I took a lawyer down a peg or two.
He said I was late and yanked my sleeve.
Going up I stopped below his floor. Out he flew.
Automatic now. I remember polishing the door
and the echo of my taps on the marble floor.

Harry Bass

I still remember the Sunday morning
he chose me for his caddy. Harry,
who wore a black patch over one eye
and swung a driver like a fly swatter,
was one of Longmeadow's token Jews
who always seemed to play together.
I cut a hole in my pocket so I could let
a new ball snake down my leg while I
walked toward the fairway from the rough
where his often landed. His partners knew
if Harry didn't. No matter how cold or grim
the day, they had come to expect we'd find
Harry's ball, as bright as a New World whose
promise hadn't faded, on the fairway's edge.

Mill Towns

When the owners chain the gates for good
and leave for Southeast Asia with a shrug,
the towns begin to fall like dominoes,
one by one. Notice the old tenements
leaning together like grandmothers
who've seen the young follow a Pied
Piper out of town and not return.
That man sitting alone in a booth
at the back of the Main Street Diner
is holding a letter from his son.
Babylon, he thinks, the Tigris River.
He'll drink the cold coffee in his cup
when the whistle calls his phantom shift.
Back in his rented room by the mill,
he'll put the letter in the old bureau
where he keeps his medals from another war.

Grey Nuns of the Sacred Heart

They blend in memory now, the kind, the good,
those who belonged behind the convent walls
down on their knees scrubbing the floors
that, if chosen, we scrubbed on Saturday
hoping to catch a glimpse of a nun with her
head uncovered. Did they really shave their heads
and kneel on shards until their knees were raw
and as bloody as a heart pierced by a lance?

What of Sister Rose of Lima, named for a saint
who wore a spiked crown concealed by roses
and slept on a bed of thorns, Sister who led us
from school to church with her hands folded
in prayer while we talked and lingered behind
before dropping off like beads from a string?

White-Tail Deer

Deer were never seen in downtown Lowell,
but that afternoon one was spotted trying
to cross the Concord River on thin ice.
No rack, so it must have been a doe.
We stood bathed in the cruiser's eerie glow
watching it slip and fall and somehow rise
and move toward the open water on the side
closest to the shore where the current's flow
was strong, and then we heard the black ice
crack. It froze, motionless as a marble statue
before with one leap it cleared the water in slow
motion. It scrambled up the bank and out of sight
between two buildings where they once made shoes,
and when the new moon rose, it was that doe.

Memoir

> *To dispel my melancholy, I write another poem.*
> —*Tu Fu*

I read that line years ago at dawn
and imagined melancholy as an old sweater
worn and thinning at the elbows,
a dark conceit to be used one day.
Today is the winter solstice.
The light barely touched the ground
when I went out to check the mail
where I found my sister's unexpected novel
and discovered that we had different fathers,
hers revealed by an aunt in her cups.
What am I to do with this image of my mother
hanged by her own hand in our basement
when I was learning how to be a soldier?
It's already pitch black to the north.
I've pulled on that sweater to keep out the cold.

Dark Hands Webbing Time

Dust coats the hotel lobby's Willard Clock.
Our church is now a shelter for the poor,
their muted voices wafting to the choir
where cots are stacked for those who dare
to sleep but never to dream. Once again
I'm a boy running home in tears from church,
my first Communion shoes bleeding in the rain,
afraid that my parents have abandoned me
to sin and the loneliness of love viewed through
a darkened screen. In a park I used to haunt
I stop to watch a baseball game. Their dark
hands webbing time, the youngest players
speak an Asian tongue. I lope across greening
grass beneath a Spaulding white as snow.

Trolls

How long after the last factory closed
the first one appeared under the bridge,
no one is certain.
People crossing would look down
and see them fishing
or smoking tobacco wrapped in brown paper.
They never seemed to leave.
There was talk.
Their wives and children quickly learned
to look away.
After all, they seldom if ever came home.
No one seems to know
when the first body appeared down river
in an eddy and then another
caught on the lip of an unused dam.
No matter how many were hooked and pulled
from the murky water, others took their places;
and like roiling high water in the spring,
they came to be expected.

Mary Shiels

Eastport, Maine

I've placed a cut branch of winterberry
on your grave and another beside the lamb
that marks your daughter's resting place.
Their berries glow like a lantern's welcome.
Who carved "a native of County Wexford,
Ireland" beneath your name for all to read?
Those words remain clear and firm after
decade after decade of wind and storm.

From where I stand at the foot of your grave,
I can see Deer Island out in the bay.
A handful of songbirds sheathed in ice
plunged into the dory of one of her
fishermen caught out in a storm last year.
He put them beneath his heavy sweater.
Only one survived the night in the makeshift
cage he placed beside his stove.
The moon that saw your birth is rising
out of the quiet bay to touch your stone.
It's Samhain Eve and time for me to go.

On Milltown Boulevard

When I left the dentist's office
a Christmas parade was passing by.
I watched a beauty queen shivering
in the back seat of a convertible,
new when shutdowns were unknown
and cars always clogged the road.
The thrift store had two tables outside
where sweaters muttered to each other.

People around me began to cheer
when a truck carrying Boy Scouts appeared.
One of the scouts had the severed head
of a coyote attached to the end of a pole.
As if to acknowledge the rising cheers,
the coyote nodded to the left and to the right.
On the truck behind the scouts', a wide-eyed
Santa Claus threw candy to the crowd.

The Flight

The sound of geese high above the house
when he woke from another restless sleep,
the sleep of the old, he told himself.
If he happened to wake during the night
when he was a child, the man across the alley
would be sitting at his kitchen table,
a man who worked in the mill with his father.
There was something ghostly about the scene:
a man in a white undershirt sitting in the
light cast by a bulb hanging from a wire;
no matter what time it was when he woke,
the man was there in that odd colorless light.
Slipping out of bed without waking his wife,
he went downstairs and then out into the yard
where he slowly raised and lowered his pale
arms until they were covered with down.

Snooker

Cigarette smoke filled the hall where he
sat with a rack in one massive hand.
He shaved his head and seldom spoke.
No one ever tried to stiff him for a game.
He was a South End Antaeus who drew
his strength from the hall and not the earth.
When a game was over, he racked the balls
with a rolling motion that sounded like thunder.

After a condemned sign was nailed to the door
and plywood nailed over every window,
a friend who had a key found him inside
curled on one of his prized snooker tables
like a child who puts his head down on the grass
to sleep. His brains were splattered over the floor.

Pheasants

They were safe from hunters in that field
high above the cemetery's fading stones,
a place where few people seemed to go.
Blackberry bushes protected it like a shield.
If I managed to get through, Mount
Wachusett's blue ghost was off to the west.
Once in that field, I was a man on a quest,
an Indian brave not making a sound.
I moved like a shadow, and when I flushed
a bird, I was startled by the sound of its wings
beating like a drum before it suddenly rose
and turned toward the brush. And then the rush
of bright feathers, the crimson mask, the ringed
neck like a band of lace, the eye pulsing and cold.

Butcher Shop

Mr. George, who wore a straw hat with
a funereal band and a white apron
speckled with blood, smiled when we came
through the door. We were cats in a ditch
when it came to our penny candy, miffed
when someone before us got the day's
last bull's eye or the only nigger babies.
A kindly butcher, he always took the fifth
when parents asked about us. To the man
now standing behind the counter, kindness
is a weakness. No candy. No Salisbury steak.
No sawdust on the floor. He sells ammunition
and sacks of food to those planning for the mess
they know must come. His hand is by a Glock.

Great Blue Heron

Far from the marsh and oxbows of Concord,
I stood on a bridge as the sun was coming up
watching a Great Blue Heron in the shallows
below an abandoned tannery that turned the water
different colors from dye that seeped from cribs.
It was the color of driftwood, motionless as stone,
ephemeral as the threads of cloud overhead
before light flooded the river and it disappeared.

I stood for a long time waiting for it to appear
in the shallows again as if it were a god returned
to tell me something. A passing truck that shook
the crumbling bridge made me turn, and when
I looked again, it was there in the shallows
with a struggling fish in its long yellow beak.

Waitresses

To all the waitresses in white blue yellow green
starched and stained uniforms for Sue Martha
Betty Joan Thelma Donna and LaDonna and for
Anne may the largest meanest shaggy honey-colored
grizzly of a brother guard you protect you and bless
you from boors who talk of life from bores who talk
of nothing from mothers who talk of daughters
who turn to drunks from drunks who turn to lovers
from preachers pimps and poets. On that last night
when your legs turn to water and water turns to stone
may he appear and opening his massive hands offer you
every tip you never got green and crisp as just picked lettuce.

Lower Belvedere

I leave my hotel before dawn to see if the tree
with the Red Sox lineup and lovers' initials,
the tree I climbed as a boy, is still there.
The streets are narrow and the houses
small pieces on a worn Monopoly board.
I'm being watched by two young women
with golden hair glowing against dark skin
who are standing on Mr. Moore's porch.

When I reach the park, I find the old beech.
I can see initials but the top is broken.
Lightning? This time I stay on the ground.
Only memory will climb to them now
Pesky and Doerr and the lovers' hearts.
"From Brazil" the hotel clerk says, "from Brazil."

Utopia

A park ranger in a Smokey the Bear hat is telling
a small group of well dressed tourists that Lowell
was once a workers' utopia where mill girls wrote
verse by candlelight and performed William Tell.
"They were" she said "admired by king and clerk,
but after the Civil War, the mills moved one by one
for cheaper labor." "It's a treasure like Yellowstone"
she says. "This city's our first Urban National Park."

"Venice of America" she says. An elderly couple
wearing light sweaters are listening from a bench
near a drained canal with more trash than water
in it. "We both worked our butts off for thirty years
in the mills," he shouts "never saw Smokey the Bear."
The ranger tugs at her sleeve. The tourists glare.

Driving North

I watch the mills and the massive clock tower
of Lawrence go past in the light of false dawn,
the day's first mask. Robert Frost's hometown.
Did he once walk its narrow streets at this hour
trying on face after face, cheerful or dour?
Mill hand or Yankee farmer close to the bone.
Walking Harvard Yard, or reading Latin alone.
Lived in poverty, or the grandson of a mill overseer.

A complicated man. Seer? I enjoy the pun. A car
full of immigrants and not the Mayflower kind
pulls beside me. I watch them out of the corner
of one eye. One tire is flat, and their muffler's
dragging on the ground. Headed for a mill?
They signal. My face is plaster. I point to the clock.

Climbing March Hill

Coos County, New Hampshire

I thought it was something Frost
might have said when one of the men,
as an aside to our conversation about
the snow that was falling so fast
you couldn't see your hand if you
held it out, said "when people from
around here die in late winter we say
they didn't make it up March Hill."
Our talk then returned to the snow.
That night after the storm had passed
I saw him at the edge of town where
the road climbs into the hills. He didn't
need a lift. The moon's long white cane
would take him as far as he needed to go.

Laundry Workers

They were the narrow-shouldered women
we saw crossing the Concord River bridge
day after day when the sun was barely up
and we were out of school for the summer.
They stood in line outside the laundry's door
waiting for the whistle to call them inside
to a long day of endless heat and steam
and a boss who might fire them for nothing.
From our hiding place across the river
where we smoked and gambled for bottle caps,
we watched them lift their weary arms
to square and fold freshly laundered sheets,
white as our sisters' first Communion dresses.
From time to time, one would hold a fresh shirt
close while she danced slowly for the others
with a grace beyond our comprehending.
Watching her move from window to window
with the shirt clinging like a ghostly lover,
we were far to young to know desire,
but we sensed the sorrow in that dancing.
A continent and half a century away,
I see them on that bridge in single file.

Ducharme

Ducharme always moved across the ring
like a massive ox yoked to a heavy plow.
He won by knockout or heard "the birdies sing"
he said. He dreamt of being another Marciano.
Ducharme saw him rock the world in Lowell
when he won the Golden Gloves, but Ducharme's
only strength was his strength. He was too slow
to duck a punch, too tough to accept the harm
punch after punch could do. A warrior-clown
who walked behind a trash truck for the city,
a beer-bellied Canuck who would not stay down.
Even flat on his back he scorned all pity.
Is he walking the streets today, or has he died?
Ducharme who sensed we live in myth not time.

Visions of Gerard at the Kerouac Monument

I'm following Gerard and Ti Jean down
Aiken Street toward the bridge. Gerard
has the tail of his mouse in a cardboard
box. His sick mouse the cat pounced upon.
"Little Kerouac mouse why didn't you run?"
They're shivering, but they must find God.
Ti Jean has questions. Is God a fist, a rod?
Saintly Gerard knows His will must be done.

I follow them across the bridge into town.
Gerard takes his brother's hand. "Ti Jean
God's a printer, like Pa, and we are his words,"
and then a lamb-white angel comes down
and sad Ti Jean wanders on alone to see
his words in stone, Gerard watching from the curb.

Lowell's Irish Mickey Ward

Round 2. Ward's left eye is already cut,
but he keeps moving toward Arturo Gatti.
My wife's gone to bed and turned out the light.
Gatti's left hook sounds like a thunderclap.
I haven't watched a fight in many years,
not since I moved away from Lowell.
A Celtic Cross glistens on Ward's shoulder.
I wince as he shakes off blow after blow.
He has my uncle Leo's fighter's face,
with features almost as flat as a stone.
Staggered by a right, he picks up the pace.
I want to see a hurt Gatti go down.
They fight to a draw. Closed eye for closed eye.
I go to bed shamefaced and stubbornly tribal.

Shadbush

On a hillside above the river that has been dammed for two centuries, Thoreau's slow moving grass-ground, my childhood river, white blossoms are opening on bushes, blossoms that once signaled the shad's return from the ocean to spawn, lavender finned, blue-green backs fading to silver, bone-hoard, that once filled weir and net and made fields green and meadows bloom. Soon blossoms will drift down and small red berries begin to form. Let the river flow.

On the Dennys River

for Gary Metras

No one waits for the tug that means a fish
has taken the fly. No voices drift

over a pool. It has been years since
salmon entered the river on the tide.

No fire rings cool on a bank.
No footprints in the frost-struck grass.

Only the gaunt shadow of a cormorant
and absence like a hook set in the heart.

Hoare's Fish Market

I walked to the market with my father
on Fridays to buy four pieces of cod
wrapped in paper soaked with grease
by the time we got back to our kitchen
where my mother and sister were waiting.
If times were good, my father bought
a piece for a neighbor who always called
it hake, or skate if he just wanted to talk.

Mr. Hoare, our Neptune in tall boots,
watched over it all: haddock and cod,
halibut and tuna, swordfish and salmon
all laid out on an endless bed of ice.
When he spoke, you heard the distant sea
with its vast multitudes that would always be.

Sunday Morning

Come down and do your crossword. I worry
when you stay in bed. Last night's early frost
killed the sweet peas but not our patch of berries.
Seven across just might be Limberlost.
The morning paper says a man with Alzheimer's
has wondered off to find his long dead wife.
He told an aide he knows just where to find her.
All he has with him is a butter knife.
Hurry down. I want to see you grimace
when you might be stumped. Five down is breath.
The day is quickly turning cold and grim.
Do you remember a Mary Elizabeth?
The raspberries in your white bowl
are bright and firm and very, very cold.

Forsythia

Ever since your surprised heart gave out
far too soon on that dark January afternoon,
I've been trying to get you down on paper:
your deep love of all that was well made,
how you could hold a rusty piece of metal
to the light and touch the hand that forged it.
You, a nurse beyond the uniform you wore,
knew the moon could pull us from our orbit
or cause the glacial earth to shudder underfoot.

A little homesick and a continent removed,
our dropped r's still clinging to us like burrs,
we shared only the Concord River when we met.
You knew its meadows, and I its final fall.
Carl, the forsythia you grew from a cutting
to replace our stunted one will bloom this year.
Standing by it, I see you drifting on our river,
water dripping slowly from your resting oars,
as the current takes you to a golden shore.

Pollywog Pond

We learned how to skate there.
Boys on black, girls on white
drawn to each other like those
small Scotty dogs on magnets
you could buy at the five and ten.
At first we could barely stand
and fell if no one held our hand,
but we soon began to skate in
circles with hands held behind
our backs the way the adults did,
or we held on at the end of a whip
knowing someone would catch us
before we tumbled to the ice.
When we sat unlacing our skates,
the moon was a clock with no hands.

At the End

A cloudless dawn. My father's about to cross
the Pawtucket Bridge below the falls.
His black hair is slicked back. His gait is firm.
My mother's riding on the back of a motorcycle
holding tight to the boy who'll become my sister's
father before he disappears like mist, but for now
the whole world is her oyster, and there's my
sister standing on one long leg before a mirror
and Aunt Irene climbing the hill to Mrs. Costello's
kitchen where she's trusted companion and servant
and I'm about to wake to the sound of heavy wagon
wheels turning on cobblestones and Goldman
the ragman singing "a-rags, a-rags, help an old man."
And no one yells "Christ-killer" from the curb.

About the Author

Tom Sexton was born in 1940 in Lowell, Massachusetts. He joined the Army out of high school and after basic training was sent to Alaska for three years. He returned to Alaska in 1968 to attend the University of Alaska in Fairbanks where he received an MFA degree. He was one of two professors who began the English Department at the newly established Anchorage campus where he taught for twenty-four years. He was appointed Professor Emeritus of English upon his retirement in 1994. Sexton was a founding editor of the *Alaska Quarterly Review* and was appointed Alaska's Poet Laureate by the Alaska State Legislature in 1995. He served in that position for eight years. Along with his wife, Sharyn, he lives in Anchorage and spends every other winter in Eastport, Maine.

THE ADASTRA PRESS LIST

1979 - 2007

Zoë Anglesey, *SOMETHING MORE THAN FORCE: Poems for Guatemala, 1971-1982,*
    letterpress, sewn, 1982, offset 1984
Margaret Key Biggs, *PETALS FROM THE WOMANFLOWER,* letterpress, sewn, 1983
Norman R. Bissell, *STRUGGLE FOR THE DAWN,* letterpress, sewn, 1982
Martha Carlson-Bradley, *BEAST AT THE HEARTH,* letterpress, sewn, 2005
Martha Carlson-Bradley, *NEST FULL OF CRIES,* letterpress, sewn, 2000
Michael Casey, *MILLRAT,* letterpress, sewn, 1996, expanded ed., offset, 1999
Michael Casey, *RAIDING A WHOREHOUSE,* letterpress, sewn, 2004
Alan Catlin, *SHELLEY AND THE ROMANTICS,* letterpress, sewn, 1993
David Chorlton, *THE VILLAGE PAINTERS,* letterpress, sewn, 1990
Leonard J. Cirino, *THE TRUTH IS NOT REAL,* letterpress, sewn, 2006
Merritt Clifton, *FROM AN AGE OF CARS,* letterpress, sewn, 1980
Clifton, Ehrhart, Sagan, Metras, *NUCLEAR QUASRTET,* letterpress, folded broadsheet,
    8.5x16", 1980
Jane Candia Coleman, *DEEP IN HIS HEART J.R. IS LAUGHING AT US,* letterpress,
    sewn, 1991
Jim Daniels, *NIAGARA FALLS,* letterpress, sewn, 1994, offset, perf. bound, 1995
Jim Daniels, *DIGGER'S BLUES,* letterpress, sewn, 2002
Jim Daniels, *DIGGER'S TERRITORY,* letterpress, sewn, 1989
Cortney Davis, *THE BODY FLUTE,* letterpress, sewn, 1994
W.D. Ehrhart, *BEAUTIFUL WRECKAGE: New & Selected Poems,* offset, perf. bound, 1999
W.D. Ehrhart, *GIFTS,* letterpress, broadsheet 9"x12", 2003
W.D. Ehrhart, *MATTERS OF THE HEART,* letterpress, sewn, 1981
W.D. Ehrhart, *MOSTLY NOTHING HAPPENS,* letterpress, sewn, 1996
W.D. Ehrhart, *THE OUTER BANKS & Other Poems,* letterpress, sewn, 1984, offset, perfect
    bound, 1984
W.D. Ehrhart, *THE DISTANCE WE TRAVEL,* letterpress, sewn, 1993, offset, perf.
    bound, 1994
W.D. Ehrhart, *SLEEPING WITH THE DEAD,* letterpress, sewn, 2006
W.D. Ehrhart, *WINTER BELLS,* letterpress, sewn, 1988
Jim Finnegan, *MY ANGELS,* letterpress, broadsheet 8.75" x 11.75", art by Susan Finnegan,
    1995
David Giannini, *ANTONIO & CLARA,* letterpress, sewn, 1990
David Giannini, *From ELLIPSES, PART II,* letterpress, broadsheet 8.75" x 11.75", 1996
Jack Gilbert, *GOING WRONG,* letterpress, broadsheet 8.75 x 11.5". 1992
Andy Gunderson, *CITY PAUSES,* letterpress, sewn, 1980
Gertrude Halstead, *memories like burrs,* letterpress, sewn, 2006, offset, sewn, 2006
Linda Lee Harper, *BLUE FLUTE,* letterpress, sewn, 1999
Michael Hettich, *BEHIND OUR MEMORIES,* letterpress, sewn, 2003
Harry Humes, *ROBBING THE PILLARS,* letterpress, sewn, 1984
Geoffrey Jacques, *SUSPENDED KNOWLEDGE,* letterpress, sewn, 1998
Greg Joly, *HAND LABOR,* letterpress, sewn, 1992
Richard Jones, *INNOCENT THINGS,* letterpress, sewn, 1985
Richard Jones, *SONNETS,* letterpress, sewn, 1990
Richard Jones, *THE STONE IT LIVES ON,* letterpress, sewn, 2000
Richard Jones, *WINDOWS AND WALLS,* letterpress, sewn, 1982
Anna Kirwan, *THE FIRST THING,* letterpress, sewn, 2001
Joseph Langland, *TWELVE POEMS with Preludes and Postludes,* letterpress, sewn, 1988,
    offset, perf. bound, 1989
M.L. Liebler, *BREAKING THE VOODOO,* letterpress, sewn, 2001
Christopher Locke, *HOW TO BURN,* letterpress, sewn, 1995
Thomas Lux, *A BOAT IN THE FOREST,* letterpress, sewn, 1992
Thomas Lux, *PECKED TO DEATH BY SWANS,* letterpress, sewn, 1993

Thomas Lux, *THE BLIND SWIMMER: Selected Early Poems, 1970-1975,* offset, perfect bound, 1996
Thomas Lux, *THE DROWNED RIVER,* offset., perf. bound, reprint, 1993
D. Roger Martin, *NO DREAMS FOR SALE,* letterpress, sewn, 1983
Dawn McDuffie, *CARMINA DETROIT,* letterpress, sewn, 2006
Gary Metras, *BIBLIOGRAPHY OF ADASTRA PRESS,* offset, sewn, 2001
Gary Metras, *DESTINY'S CALENDAR,* offset, perfect bound, reprint, 1988
Gary Metras, *SEAGULL BEACH,* letterpress, sewn, 1995
Gary Metras, ed., *THE ADASTRA READER,* offset, perfect bound, 1987
Gary Metras, *THE NECESSITIES,* letterpress, sewn, 1979
Gary Metras, *THE NIGHT WATCHES,* letterpress, sewn, 1981
Michael Miller, *EACH DAY,* letterpress, sewn, 2005
Judith Neeld, *SEA FIRE,* letterpress, sewn, 1987
Ed Ochester, *ALLEGHENY,* letterpress, sewn, 1995
Ed Ochester, *COOKING IN KEY WEST,* letterpress, sewn, 2000
Ed Ochester, *THE REPUBLIC OF LIES,* letterpress, sewn, 2007
Peter Oresick, *OTHER LIVES,* letterpress, sewn, 1985, offset, perf. 1985
Stephen Philbrick, *THREE,* letterpress, sewn, 2003
Stephen Philbrick, *UP TO THE ELBOW,* letterpress, sewn, 1997
Constance Pierce, *PHILIPPE AT HIS BATH,* letterpress, sewn, 1983
David Raffeld, *INTO THE WORLD OF MEN,* letterpress, sewn, 1997
Davidd Raffeld, *THE BALLAD OF HARMONICA GEORGE and Other Poems,* letterpress, sewn, 1989
Michael Rattee, *MENTIONING DREAMS,* letterpress, sewn, 1985
Michael & Kiev Rattee, *ENOUGH SAID: A Poetic Dialogue Between Father & Son,* letterpress, sewn, 2002
Susan Edwards Richmond, *BOTO,* letterpress, sewn, 2002
Susan Edwards Richmond, *PURGATORY CHASM,* letterpress, sewn, 2007
Karen Rigby, *FESTIVAL BONE,* letterpress, sewn, 2004
Becky Rodia, *ANOTHER FIRE,* letterpress, sewn, 1997
Miriam Sagan, *ACEQUIA MADRE: Through the Mother Ditch,* letterpress, sewn, 1988
Miriam Sagan, *POCAHONTAS DISCOVERS AMERICA,* letterpress, sewn, 1993
Charles Scott, *OLD ORDNANCE,* letterpress, sewn, 2005
Tom Sexton, *A CLOCK WITH NO HANDS,* offset, perfect bound, 2007
Tom Sexton, *LEAVING FOR A YEAR,* letterpress, sewn, 1998
Tom Sexton, *THE LOWELL POEMS,* letterpress, sewn, 2005
Laurel Speer, *DON'T DRESS YOUR CAT IN AN APRON,* letterpress, sewn, 1981
Barry Sternlieb, *FISSION,* letterpress, sewn, 1986
Wally Swist, *ACCOMPANIMENT,* letterpress, broadsheet 8.5" x 11", 2003
Wally Swist, *FOR THE DANCE,* letterpress, sewn, 1991
Wally Swist, *WAKING UP THE DUCKS,* letterpress, sewn, 1987
Susan Terris, *POETIC LICENSE,* letterpress, sewn, 2004
Emmet Van Driesche, *THE LAND BEFORE US,* letterpress, sewn, 2004

❖

Though many of these titles are limited editions and are out of print, inquiries about copies may be obtained from the publisher, through your book store, and various online sources.